PROVERBS & SAYINGS OF IRELAND

The words of the wise and their dark sayings
(Book of Proverbs)

The proverb cannot be bettered
(Irish Proverb)

When a fool is told a proverb, its meaning has to be
explained to him
(Ashanti Proverb)

PROVERBS & SAYINGS OF IRELAND

Edited by
Sean Gaffney & Seamus Cashman

First published 1974
Paperback edition 1976
© 1974 The Wolfhound Press
All rights reserved
This edition 1978

Published by
Wolfhound Press
98 Ardilawn, Portmarnock,
County Dublin.
Phone 452162.

ISBN 0 9503454 0 7
ISBN 0 9503454 4 X (Paperback)

Printed and bound in the Republic of Ireland

CONTENTS

25 illustrations by Billy Merwick

ACKNOWLEDGEMENTS

We acknowledge with gratitude the contributions and encouragement of many friends, in particular our parents, Ann and James Cashman, and Margaret Gaffney. A special word of thanks to Margaret Ryan, Deirdre Duffy, Monica Miller, Joy Adams, John Logue and Paul Walsh.

CLASSIFICATIONS

Ability
Advice
Affectation
Age
Anger
Appearance
Art
As....as...
Beauty
Betrayer
Bitterness
Blessings
Boasting
Borrowing
Bravery
Bribery
Carelessness
Caution
Change
Character
Charity
Chastity
Children
Choice
Clergy
Coincidence
Comfort
Compromise
Contentment
Conversation
Courtship
Criticism
Cunning
Curses
Cynicism
Danger
Death

Debt
Deception
Delusion
Desire
Despair
Devil
Discipline
Dismissal
Drink
Economy
Education
Effort
Egotism
Eloquence
Endurance
English, The
Equality
Error
Evil
Excused
Experience
Fair-haired
Fame
Familiarity
Fate
Fear
Fighting
Flattery
Flimsiness
Food
Fool
Foolishness
Forgiveness
Fortune
Frail
Freedom
Friendship

Futility
Gambling
Generosity
Gentleness
God
Goodness
Gossip
Gratitude
Greed
Grief
Happiness
Health
Home
Honesty
Honour
Hope
Humility
Humour
Hunger
Idleness
Ignorance
Impossibility
Independence
Inequality
Initiative
Intelligence
Involvement
Irishman
Judgement
Justice
Kerry
Kindness
Kinship
Knowledge
Law
Laziness
Leadership

CLASSIFICATIONS

Lies
Life
Love
Luck
Manners
Marriage
Maturity
Meanness
Men
Misfortune
Mother
Nature
Neatness
Necessity
Nobility
Obedience
Obligation
Ownership
Participation
Patience
Patriotism
Peace
Perception
Pity
Poetry
Possession
Poverty
Power
Presumption
Pride
Procrastination
Promise
Proverbs
Prudence
Red-hair
Repentance
Reputation

Revenge
Rogue
Rumour
Scarcity
Seasons
Secret
Self-destruction
Selfishness
Sense
Separation
Shame
Shyness
Silence
Strength
Stupidity
Success
Suitability
Tact
Talent
Talkativeness
Thrift
Time
Treachery
Trouble
Trust
Truth
Understanding
Uselessness
Value
Vanity
Warning
Wastefulness
Wealth
Weather
Welcome
Widow
Wisdom

Women
Work
Youth

INTRODUCTION

'The proverb cannot be bettered'; 'though the proverb is
abandoned, it cannot be falsified'. How true these are the
reader will best discover for himself in the following
collection of Irish proverbs, sayings and triads. The triad is
perhaps the most fascinating type of saying and though
little heard today in the non-Irish speaking parts of the
country, it is still to be heard in the Gaeltacht areas,
especially in West Cork, West Galway and the Aran Islands.
   A glance through the index of key words reveals the
range of the Irish proverb, its themes, and the imagery and
symbols used. As might be expected, the reputed vulner-
ability of our race to religion and romanticism is well
represented. But the story the proverb tells is not quite
that of a priest-ridden peasantry content in their poverty.
Rather it shows us to have — or at least to have had — a
subtle, sly perhaps, but generally humorous self-
confidence. 'The priest's pig' may get 'the most porridge';
but the proverb also advises us to be 'neither intimate nor
distant with the clergy'! Nor are we shown to be wholly
susceptible to romanticism: 'it's better to be lucky than to
be an early riser' but 'there's no success without authority
and laws'. The proverbs reveal a deep conviction in a
relationship between the spiritual and the material that is
both challenging and realistic.
   Proverbs are, in a sense, a race's unconscious expression
of its moral attitudes. Our proverbs seem frequently to
take the form of a national confession of sins: the evils of
drink, gambling, greed, vanity, improvidence abound. But
the virtues are there: faith, gentleness, love of nature,

9

tolerance, and a trust in a life after death that offers a constant check to the materialism already mentioned.

Irish proverbs are rich in nature symbolism and imagery: the wind, the sea, the mountains; plants, animals, birds and fishes. The kingfisher, mackerel, thistle, plover, the horse and the hare, even the common crow are all called upon to mirror our achievements, hopes and failings.

While the proverbs of a race are often readily identifiable as belonging to that race, the ideas expressed and the images used touch on matters more fundamental than a national identity. One can readily accept that Irish proverbs should have their exact counterparts among the proverbs of other Celtic races. There are numerous examples of similarities among the sayings of the Irish, Welsh and Scottish — A long illness doesn't lie (Irish); To be long sick and to die nevertheless (Welsh); Marriage at the dungheap and the Godparents far away (Irish); Marriage o'er the anvil, sponsorship o'er the sea (Scottish); A drink is shorter than a story (Irish and Manx); Bribery splits a stone (Irish); Envy splits a stone (Scottish). Such typical proverbs as these listed here also have their counterparts in most European languages.

However, it is interesting to discover that our proverbs also have affinities with those of races as far distant as the West Indies and Africa. Among Jamaican blacks, who are of African descent, there is a saying: 'When you sleep wid darg, you ketch him flea'. Our equivalent is: 'He who lies with dogs rises with fleas'. We speak of sending the goose on a message to the foxes' den; the Hausa of West Africa have: 'Even if the hyena's town is destroyed, one does not send a dog in to trade'.

Irish proverbs and saying derive from two mainstreams: the gaelic tradition, in the Irish language, and the anglo-Irish tradition, in the English language. Both reflect the strong biblical influence found in the proverbs throughout 'western' countries. This collection includes some of the oldest seanfhocail (old-sayings) recorded in Ireland as well as sayings of more recent origin. But it is by no means exhaustive. The exact origins of most of these sayings are unknown: perhaps a throw-away phrase; perhaps a line of a poem long forgotten - who knows? It is what survives that matters.

For readers interested in pursuing the Irish Proverb further, a brief word on some sources. Several substantial collections have been published (from which many in this collection have been taken, and which we gratefully acknowledge.) Most of these are unfortunately long out of print. The most recent, and certainly the finest is T. S. O'Maille, ed., *Sean-fhocala Chonnacht,* 2 vols. (Dublin, 1948-52). Others are: T. O'Donoghue, ed., *Sean-fhocail na Mumhain,* a Gaelic League publication, 1902; E. Ua Muirgheasa, ed., *Sean fhocla Uladh,* (1907) which contains English translations as does T. F. O'Rahilly, *A Miscellany of Irish Proverbs,* (Dublin, 1922). Shorter collections will be found in J. O'Daly, *Irish Language Miscellany,* Burke, *Irish Grammar;* Hardiman, *Irish Minstrelsy,* 2 vols. reissued by IUP in 1969; the *Gaelic Journal* and *The Ulster Journal of Archaeology.* P. W. Joyce, *English as we Speak it in Ireland,* (Dublin, 1910) is a useful and entertaining starting point though of limited use for proverbs. Two important sources still to be fully researched are the Douglas Hyde 'Diaries' in the National Library of Ireland, and the manuscript collections of the Irish Folklore Department in UCD, in particular the 'Schools Mss.' for anglo-Irish proverbs. *Bealoideas* the journal of the Folklore Commission includes lists of proverbs in its various issues. Information on further sources will be found in bibliographies in the published works mentioned.

Most of the proverbs in this collection have been translated from the Irish language. English translations of proverbs in the Irish language are not always successful. We have endeavoured to remain as close to the original as possible. An illustration of the effects of translation, however, can be readily seen by comparing 'One beetle recognises another' with the original Irish proverb 'Aithnionn ciarog ciarog eile'. The impact of the expression depends greatly on the sound of the word ciarog, and its repetition. The pattern cannot be reproduced satisfactorily in English; and the word 'beetle' is by comparison with the Irish word, weak and ineffectual.

We have classified each proverb by subject recognising that such classification is both limiting and subjective. For proverbs are by their very nature elusive and usually defy adequate classification under any one heading. However as the index contains the key-words of each proverb, our arrangement should cause the reader little difficulty.

PROVERBS & SAYINGS

PROVERBS & SAYINGS OF IRELAND

Ability

No one can tell what he is able to do till he tries	1
You can't whistle and chew meal at the same time	2
You can't bark and run at the same time	3
A vessel only holds its fill	4
Often the hound that was made fun of killed the deer	5
The strong man may when he wants to; the weak man when he's able	6
The gobadan (kingfisher) cannot work both tides	7

Advice

Don't give cherries to pigs; don't give advice to a fool	8
A man is often a bad adviser to himself and a good adviser to another	9
The man who won't have advice will have conflict	10
He is bad that will not take advice, but he is a thousand times worse that takes every advice	11
The cat is his own best adviser	11a
Crafty advice is often got from a fool	12
A wise man takes advice	13

Affectation

A ring on her finger and not a stitch of clothes on her back	14
Sparing at home and lavish in the hospital	15
Like the sun on the hill-top, but like a thistle on the hearth	16
Street angel, house devil	17

Age

Anger

Appearance

Art

As...

A localised Kerry expression. When the Irish
were being hunted down in Penal times a
particularly vicious duo, a Captain Barrington
and Colonel Nelson used a bloodhound to chase
their quarry which savaged the victim terribly,
hence giving rise to the saying.

A Cork expression. The story goes that the goat
belonged to Atwell Hayes who was father of
Sir Henry Hayes, sherrif of Cork in 1790. The
goat was reputed to be old even when Atty was
a young man. A generation later Captain Philip
Allen, son-in-law of Sir Henry Hayes became
mayor of Cork, (in 1800) and gave a civil
banquet to celebrate the occasion. At this time
the goat died and Allen being a bit of a joker
served up the hind quarters of the goat
unknowingly to his guests, as venison. The
'venison' was proclaimed by the city fathers as
delicious. In county Armagh the corresponding
expression is 'As old as Killylea bog'.

As wise as the women of Mungret   45
   A Limerick expression. The very amusing story
   attached to this saying concerns the monastic
   foundation and school at Mungret. A number of
   scholars was sent from Cashel to compete with
   their Mungret counterparts. However the
   Limerick scholars fearing defeat and the loss of
   their reputation dressed as washerwomen and
   waited along the roadside, washing in the nearby
   river. As the Cashel contingent approached and
   asked the 'women' for directions they were
   completely taken aback when answered in
   perfect Greek. Thinking that if the washerwomen
   were so learned then the scholars must be
   unusually brilliant, the poor Tipperary monks
   turned for home, leaving the reputation of
   Mungret intact and untarnished!

As hard as the hob of hell   46

As cunning as the fox   47

As long as a wet Sunday   48

As old as the hills   49

As bald as a buailtin *(see notes)*   50

As sharp as a ciotog *(see notes)*   51

As bitter as thick milk   52

As crooked as a ram's horn   53

As brown as a berry   54

As big as a smith's meitheal *(see notes)*   55

As sharp as the word of a fool   56

As sharp as the teeth of a hound   57

As wet as dung   58

As pretty as a May flower   59

As old as the Cailleach Beare *(see notes)*   60

As fresh as a daisy   61

As bright as a lily   62

As slow as a late dinner	63
As dull as ditchwater	64
As swift as a hare	65
As true as the gospel	66
As deep as the sea	67
As bashful as a girl	68
As treacherous as an Englishman	69
As melodious as a lark	70
As brave as Fionn MacCumhall *(see notes)*	71
As yellow as a ragweed (ragworth)	72
As lazy as a donkey	73
As lazy as a piper's luidin (little finger)	73a
As busy as a bee	74
As salty as the sea	75
As good as gold	76
As rich as Damer	77

A Dublin expression, not in common usage.
The story is based on Joseph Damer who was
born in 1630. After serving Cromwell he
returned to Ireland where he purchased much
land forfeited in the Williamite confiscations.
He became a banker and achieved much
notoriety as a miser. He died in 1720 leaving
nearly half a million pounds, a phenomenal
amount even by to-day's standards. Jonathan
Swift was moved, as was his wont, to comment
unfavourably on Mr. Damer:
The ghost of old Damer who left not his betters
When it heard of a bank appear'd to his debtors
And lent them for money the backs of his letters
His debtors they wonder'd to find him so frank,
For old Nick gave the papers the mark of the bank.

As hairy as a puck-goat's head	77a
As thieving as a fox's snout	77b

PROVERBS & SAYINGS OF IRELAND

Beauty

Betrayer

Bitterness

Blessings

Change

Character

Charity

Chastity

Children

Criticism

Cunning

Curses

Cynicism

Danger

Death

Debt

Deception

Delusion

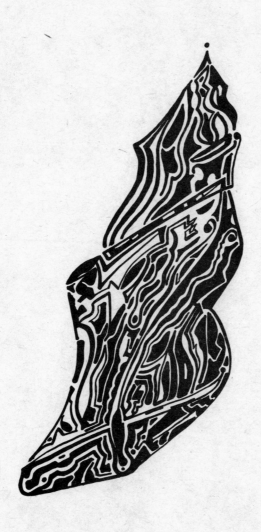

Excuses

Experience

Fair-haired

Fame

Familiarity

Fate

What kills one man gives life to another   335

About the foot of the tree the foliage falls   336

Fear

Fear is a fine spur, so is rage   337

Be afraid, and you'll not meet danger   338

The man who is struck on the head, will
  afterwards be afraid   339

Fighting

To fight like Kilkenny cats   340
> In 1798 when the Hessians were quartered
> in Kilkenny they amused themselves by tying
> two cats tails together and throwing them over
> a line, to fight. Their officer on hearing of this,
> ordered his men to stop. However the soldiers
> continued the practice in secret, and one day
> while they were amusing themselves in this
> manner they heard the officer approaching.
> One soldier drawing his sword cut down the
> cats leaving only their tails hanging. When the
> officer enquired as to where the cats were, the
> soldier replied that the cats had fought so
> furiously that they had devoured all but each
> other's tails. The story proved immensely
> popular and achieved widespread fame, but it
> is probably just a tall tale!

Quarrelsome dogs get dirty coats   341

Don't kick till you're spurred   342

Be warning but not striking   343

A word goes to the wind but a blow goes to the
  bones   344

Wine is better than blood   345

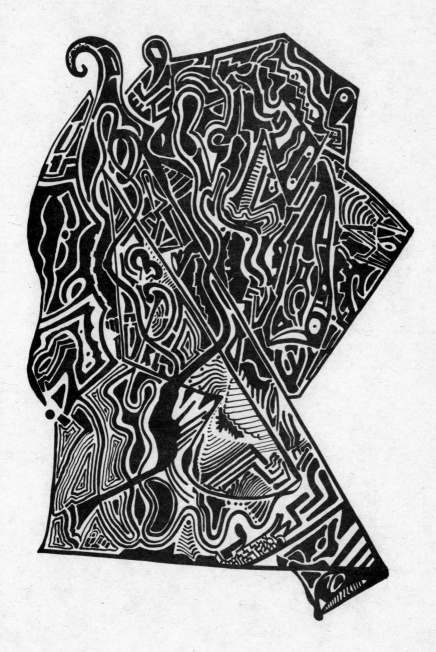

PROVERBS & SAYINGS OF IRELAND

The lucky man awaits prosperity, the unlucky man gives a blind leap — 380

Let each person judge his own luck, good or bad — 381

Frail

The point of a rush would draw blood from his cheek — 382

Freedom

Let every man have his own world — 383

You can take the horse to the well, but you can't make him drink — 384

Friendship

No war is as bitter as a war between friends, but it doesn't last long — 385

Reverence ceases once blood is spilled — 386

Two persons never lit a fire without disagreeing — 387

If you will walk with lame men you will soon limp yourself — 388

There was never a scabby sheep in a flock that didn't like to have a comrade — 389

The man long absent is forgotten — 390

In times of trouble friends are recognised — 391

A friend's eye is a good mirror — 392

Reckoning up is the ending of friendship — 393

The friend that can be bought is not worth buying — 394

If I like the sow I like her litter — 395

Futility

Gambling

It is the hope of recompense that ruins the card-player	433
Better a son a gambler than a drinker	434
The expectation of success is what beggars the gambler	435

Generosity

A big belly was never generous	436
A generous man, they say, has never gone to hell	437
Wide is the door of the little cottage	438
As you have burned the candle, give the inch	439
Take gifts with a sigh, most men give to be paid	440
O'Neill's gift and his two eyes looking after it *(see notes)*	441
It is worth going to meet generosity that is slow	442

Gentleness

A gentle answer quenches anger	443
A kind word never broke anyone's mouth	444

God

God's help is nearer than the door	445
God is not as severe as he is said to be	446
God often pays debts without money	447
God moves slowly yet his grace comes	448
God never closes one door but he opens another	449
God shares the good things	450
The person not taught by God is not taught by man	451

Goodness

Gossip

Gratitude

Sit on your heel and thank goodness for a new stool	470
You can't examine the teeth of a gift horse	471
Eaten bread is soon forgotten	472
I think little of buttermilk when I'm full of it	473
Strike a dog with a bone and he'll not growl	474
Thank God the right side of the house is out	475

Greed

One cannot take out of a sack more than the full of it	476
If the cat had a churn her paw would often be in it	477
Though honey is sweet, do not lick it off a briar	478
The covetous man is always in want	479
He's not covetous but he'd fain have all	480
Don't refuse to sell your horse for the sake of a crown	481
Eating and complaining like the greedy hen	482
A rag on every bush	483
Too many irons in the fire	484
A finger in every pie	485

Grief

The most recent grief is the heaviest	486
No grief at feasts	487
From strong relationships often comes great grief	488

There is no cure for grief but to put it under
    your foot   489

Happiness

Health

Home

There is no fireside like your own fireside	509
It's a long way from home that the plover cries	509a

Honesty

When rogues disagree, honest men get their own	510
The man that steals stacks thinks all the world thieves	511
The miller's pigs are fat but God knows whose meal they ate	512
He is as honest as the priest	513

Honour

A patch is better than a hole, but a hole is more honourable than a patch	514
It's more difficult to maintain honour than to become prosperous	515
A man may live after losing his life but not after losing his honour	516
Honour is more precious than gold	517

Hope

Live horse and you'll get grass	518
Hope soothes the tired heart	519
Hope is the physician of each misery	520
Face the sun but turn your back to the storm	521
There's no flood that doesn't recede	522
Do not expect more than you deserve	523

Idleness

Ignorance

Impossibility

Independence

Inequality

Initiative

Judgement

Justice

Kerry

Kerry security: bond, pledge, oath, and keep
    the money   574

Kindness

Pressure of business weakens kindness   575

The old hag is the better of being warmed, but
    the worse of being burned   576

Kinship

One beetle recognises another   577

Blood is stronger than water   578

One chafer knows another   579

One thief knows another   580

One pig knows another   581

One liar knows another   582

Great minds live apart; people may meet, but
    mountains and rocks never   583

Knowledge

A blind dog won't bark at the moon   584

A book to a blind man signifies nothing   585

Better knowledge of the evil, than the evil
    without knowledge   586

The person with least knowledge talks most   587

Law

Laziness

Leadership

Lies

Life

Love

Love hides ignominy and evil	624
Love is no impartial judge	625
House without hound, cat, or child, house without love or affection	626
Love a woman or a child without their knowing it	627
To the raven her own chick is white	628
What is nearest the heart is usually nearest the lips	629
What is nearest the heart comes out	630
Love cools quickly	631
Love conceals ugliness, and hate sees a lot of faults	632
She who fills the heart, fills the eye	633
There's no love until there's a family	634
Absence makes the heart grow fond	635

Luck

It's better to be lucky than to be an early riser	636
A chance shot will not kill the devil	637
The man who has luck in the morning has luck in the afternoon	638
There's luck in sharing	639
It's better to be lucky than wise	640
A meeting in the sunlight is lucky, and a burying in the rain	641
The lucky person has only to be born	642
Luck seldom lasts	643

Manners

Without store no friends; without rearing no manners	644
Better good manners than good looks	645

Marriage

The husband of the sloven is known in the field amidst a crowd	646
A growing moon and a flowing tide are lucky times to marry in	647
Never make a toil of pleasure, as the man said when he dug his wife's grave only three feet deep	648
Marriage at the dungheap and the godparents far away	649
Woe to him who does not heed a good wife's counsel	650
It's why women marry.........the creatures, God bless them, are too shy to say no	651
There was never an old slipper but there was an old stocking to match it	652
A young man is bothered till he's married, after that he's bothered entirely	653
There's only one thing in the world better than a good wife...no wife	654
The dowry falls over the cliff; but the protruding lip remains on the wife	655
A bad wife takes advice from everyone but her own husband	656
He breaks his wife's head and then buys a plaster for it	657
There are no trials till marriage	658
The carefree mother's daughter makes a bad wife	659

It's a lonesome washing that there's not a (man's) shirt in 660

Marry a mountainy woman and you'll marry the mountain 661

She's a good woman, but she didn't take off her boots yet 662

The day you marry your wife you marry your children 663

The blanket is the warmer of being doubled 664

She burnt her coal and did not warm herself 665

He married money and got a woman with it 666

Marry in haste and be sorry at your leisure 667

Maturity

By age or ability you're no child 668

Meanness

What you give wouldn't blind the eye of a midge 669

As tight as tuppence in a market-woman's trashbag 670

If you give the loan of your britches, don't cut off the buttons 671

'Tis strange that the man who is so quick to find fault is himself so stingy about food 672

To come with one hand longer than the other 673

Nothing comes into a closed hand 674

Men

Some men are like bagpipes...they can't speak till their bellies are filled 675

Misfortune

Mother

Nature

You won't get from a cat but its skin	689
The lamb is a sheep in the long run	690
Its nature breaks out through the eyes of the cat	691
Let the tail go with the hide	692
A wild goose never laid a tame egg	693
What can you expect from a pig but a grunt	694
How could the apple be but like the apple tree	695
Nature is stronger than nurture	696
He got it from nature as the pig got the rooting in the ground	697
Often a cow does not take after its breed	698
What would a young cat do but eat mice?	699
Nature will come through the claws, and the hound will follow the hare	700
If you put a silk dress on a goat he is a goat still	701
Every bird as it is reared and the lark for the bog	702
What is in the marrow is hard to take out of the bone	703
The wood will renew the foliage it sheds	704
What will come from the briar but the berry	705
The hand goes only where the leg goes	706

Neatness

A handstaff of holly, a buailtin of hazel, a single sheaf and a clean floor *(see notes)*	707

Necessity

One who is without cows must be his own dog	708

Nobility

Obedience

Keep your tongue in your jaw and your toe
in your pump   714

Obligation

Pity the man who has a stranger's spancel on him   715

Ownership

To every cow its calf; to every book its copy   716
(see notes)

PROVERBS & SAYINGS OF IRELAND

Participation

Patience

Patriotism

Peace

A wren in the hand is better than a crane to be
caught 747

Possession satisfies 748

A bird in the hand is worth two in the bush 749

It's better than the loan you couldn't get 750

Half a loaf is better than no bread 751

A live dog is better than a dead lion 752

A trout in the pot is better than a salmon in the
sea 753

Poverty

Put a beggar on horseback and he'll ride to hell 754

Put a beggar on horseback and he'll go on a gallop 755

Poverty parts good company 756

Poverty destroys companionship 757

Many a defect is seen in the poor man 758

It's hard to take britches off bare hips 759

The full man does not understand the wants of
the hungry 760

A little pleases a poor man 761

Poor men take to the sea; the rich to the
mountains 762

Poverty creates sadness 763

Pity the man who does wrong and is poor as well 764

There is nothing in the world so poor as going
to hell 765

The thief is no danger to the beggar 766

Poverty is no shame 767

Two things that go to loss....turf on a mountain
and the wisdom of a poor man 768

Shame is ever a part of poverty 769

No-one is ever poor who has the sight of his eyes
and the use of his feet 770

There is no tune without a penny 771

A poor man never yet lost his property 772

Poor is the church without music 773

A smoky cabin, a handful of spuds and a
flea-filled bed 774

Power

No stopping the force of a going wheel by hand 775

No forcing the sea 776

Presumption

Don't count your chickens before they are
hatched 777

Don't bless the fish till it gets to the land 778

Don't build the sty until the litter comes 779

Praise the ripe field not the green corn 780

Praise the ford when you have crossed it 781

You must empty a box before you fill it again 782

Pride

The pride of women and the pride of priests 783

It is difficult to soothe the proud 784

Pride comes before a fall 785

Pride feels no pain 786

Pride is the author of every sin 787

The jump of a cock on the dungheap 788

Procrastination

There is no virtue in the herb that is not got
in time   789

A postponement till morning a postponement
for ever   790

It is no time to go for the doctor when the
patient is dead   791

Promise

A promise is a debt   792

Proverbs

Proverbs cannot be contradicted   793

The proverb cannot be bettered   794

Though the proverb is abandoned, it is not
falsified   795

Prudence

Don't throw out the dirty water until you have
the clean water in   796

It's better to return from the centre of the ford
than drown in the flood   797

The sty before the litter   798

Red-hair

If you meet a red-haired woman, you'll meet a
crowd   799

To be red-haired is better than to be without a
head   800

Repentance

To put off repentance is dangerous   801

It's better to be sorry and stay than to be sorry
and go away   802

Reputation

It's a small thing that outlives a man   803

Remember even if you lose all, keep your good
name for if you lose that you are worthless   804

Those who get the name of rising early may lie
all day   805

When a man gets his feet in lime he cannot
easily get rid of it   806

Revenge

No dealing with a revengeful man   807

Rogue

He was never good since the time a yard (of cloth)
made a coat for him   808

Don't mention him and a decent man in the
one day   809

A sly rogue is often in good dress   810

She would drink the cream and say the cat she
   had was an old rogue   811

The horse with the most scars is the one that
   highest kicks his rear   812

Rumour

The person who brings a story to you will take
   away two from you   813

A story without an author is not worth
   listening to   814

Leave the bad tale where you found it   815

There is no smoke without fire   816

(See also **Gossip**)

Scarcity

When all fruits fail welcome haws	817
When the fruit is scarcest, its taste is sweetest	818
We have a fine day more often than a kiln-cast	819

Seasons

A soft-dropping April brings milk to cows and sheep	820
Autumn days come quickly like the running of a hound on the moor	821
A misty winter brings a pleasant spring, a pleasant winter a misty spring	822
Many a sudden change takes place on a spring day	823
In winter the milk goes to the cow's horns	824

Secret

A secret is a weapon and a friend	825
It is no secret that is known to three	826
Fences (ditches) have ears	827
Don't tell your secret even to a fence	828
Woe to the man that entrusts his secrets to a ditch	829
The secret of an old woman scolding	830
If it's a secret, it's binding	831
Don't tell secrets to the children of your relatives	832

Self-Destruction

No tree but has rotten wood enough to burn it   833

A man may be his own ruin   834

A wedge from itself splits the oak tree   835

A man has often cut a rod to beat himself   836

Selfishness

It's for her own good that the cat purrs   837

His own wound is what everyone feels soonest   838

What is nearest the heart is nearest the mouth   839

He who is best to me is he who shall get the
     best share   840

The full stomach does not understand the
     empty one   841

The man who was dividing Ireland didn't leave
     himself last   842

Sense

Sense doesn't come before age   843

Separation

After the gathering comes the scattering   844

Shame

What would shame him would turn back a
     funeral   845

A fist full of gain and a village full of shame   846

Success

Suitability

Tact

Better sit beside him than in his place	867
A short visit is best and that not too often	868
The eye should be blind in the home of another	869
It's often a man's mouth broke his nose	870
Don't say everything you want to say lest you hear something you would not like to hear	871
Don't let your tongue cut your throat	872
See not what you see and hear not what you hear	873
Never speak to the feet while the head is alive	874
Don't rest your eyes beyond what is your own	875
It's bad manners to talk about ropes in the house of a man whose father was hanged	876

Talent

A greyhound finds food in its feet	877
The slow hound often has good qualities	878
The bird that can sing and won't sing should be made to sing	879
A cat between two houses, a rabbit between two holes, the two liveliest	879a

Talkativeness

Great talk and little action	880
Do not be talkative in an alehouse	881
You kissed the blarney stone	882

PROVERBS & SAYINGS OF IRELAND

Thrift

Time

Treachery

Trouble

Trust

Truth

A man with a loud laugh makes truth itself seem folly	895
Truth is great and will win out	896
Even the truth may be bitter	897
There are two tellings to every story	898
Drunkenness and anger, 'tis said tell the truth	899
What I'm afraid to hear I'd better say first myself	900
Truth speaks even though the tongue were dead	901
You can keep away from the rogue, but you cannot keep yourself safe from the liar	902
Truth stands when everything else falls	903
It is no shame to tell the truth	904
Tell the truth and shame the devil	905

Understanding

The well-filled belly has little understanding of the empty	906
'Tis afterwards that everything is understood	907

Uselessness

It's a bad hound that's not worth the whistling	908
He knows how many grains to a bushel of wheat	909
He knows the price of everything and the value of nothing	910
He couldn't drag a herring off the coals	911
It's just a wisp in place of a brush	912

Value

One pair of good soles is worth two pairs of upper leathers	913
Without pressing too little or too hard, hold tight the reins for he's a fool who would not get value from a borrowed horse	914
It's not worth a cuckoo-spit	915
Better an idle house than a bad tenant	916

Vanity

Pity him who makes his opinion a certainty	917
He thinks that he himself is the very stone that was hurled at the castle	918
He dotes on his midden and thinks it the moon	919

Warning

That's a spoon ye'll sup sorrow with yet   920

Wastefulness

Wilful waste makes woeful want   921

Wealth

A shamefaced man seldom acquires wealth   922
The money-maker (profiteer) is never tired   923
The doorstep of a great house is slippery   924
There is misfortune only where there is wealth   925
Sweet is the voice of the man who has wealth   926
A hut is a palace to a poor man   927
A heavy purse makes a light heart   928
There's little value in the single cow   929
A man of one cow—a man of no cow   930
It's easy to knead when meal is at hand   931

Weather

Wind from the east is good for neither man nor
beast   932
A Kerry shower is of twenty-four hours   933
Better April showers than the breadth of the ocean
in gold   934

Welcome

Better for a man to have even a dog welcome
him than bark at him   935

Going in is not the same as coming out   936
A welcome is a debtor's face   937

Widow

What's all the world to a man when his wife is
   a widow   938

Wisdom

A wise head keeps a shut mouth   939
Everyone is wise till he speaks   940
Food is no more important than wisdom   941
A contraction (in writing) is enough for a scholar   942
The beginning of wisdom is the fear of God   943
There's no wise man without a fault   944
He may die of wind but he'll never die of wisdom   945
You can't put a wise head on young shoulders   946
Wisdom is what makes a poor man a king,
   a weak person powerful, a good generation
   of a bad one, a foolish man reasonable   947
Though wisdom is good in the beginning, it is
   better at the end   948
A little of anything isn't worth a pin; but a wee
   bit of sense is worth a lot   949
No making of a wise man   950

Women

A dishonest woman can't be kept in and an
   honest woman won't   951

There is no thing wickeder than a woman of
    evil temper   952

A bad woman (wife) drinks a lot of her own bad
    butter-milk   953

A foolish woman knows a foolish man's faults   954

A whistling woman and a crowing hen will bring
    no luck to the house they are in   955

Beef to the heels like a Mullingar heifer   956

Eight lives for the men and nine for the women   957

Wherever there are women there's talking, and
    wherever there's geese there's cackling   958

Irishwomen have a dispensation from the Pope
    to wear the thick ends of their legs downwards   959

Women are shy and shame prevents them from
    refusing a man   960

Everything dear is a woman's fancy   961

Like an Irish wolf she barks at her own shadow   962

She wipes the plate with the cat's tail   963

More hair than tit, like a mountain heifer   964

Women are stronger than men, they do not die
    of wisdom   965

When the old woman is hard pressed, she has
    to run   966

It's difficult to trust a woman   967

Man to the hills, woman to the shore   968

Beat a woman with a hammer and you'll have gold   969

'Tis as hard to see a woman cry, as a goose go
    barefoot   970

'Where comes a cow,' the wise man lay down
    (St Colmcille), 'there follows a woman, and
    where comes a woman follows trouble'   971

Only a fool would prefer food to a woman   972

Don't be ever in a court or a castle without a
 woman to make your excuse   973

An excuse is nearer to a woman than her apron   974

There is nothing sharper than a woman's tongue   975

A woman without is she who has neither pipe nor
 child   976

The yellow praiseach (kale) of the fields that brings
 the Meath women to harm   977

A woman like a goose, a sharp pecking woman
A woman like a pig, a sleepy-headed woman
A woman like a sickle, a strong stubborn woman
A woman like a goat, a woman of rushing visits
A woman like a sheep, an affable friendly woman
A woman like a lamb, a quiet friendly woman   978

It is not the most beautiful woman who has the
 most sense   979

A woman can beat the devil   980

A shrew gets her wish but suffers in the getting   981

Work

Many a time the man with ten (cows) has
 overtaken the man with forty (cows)   982

Do it as if there was fire in your skin   983

The seeking for one thing will find another   984

Make your hay before the fine weather leaves you   985

Sow early and mow early   986

The early riser gets through his business but
 not through early rising   987

The slow horse reaches the mill   988

Making the beginning is one third of the work   989

The quiet pigs eat all the draff   990

The sweat of one's brow is what burns everyone   991

Everyone lays a burden on the willing horse   992

Every little makes a mickle   993

Speed and accuracy do not agree   994

Never put off tomorrow what you can do today   995

I'll go there tonight for evening is speedier than
  morning   996

The person of the greatest talk is the person of
  the least work   997

Be there with the day and be gone with the day   998

About evening a man is known   999

Long churning makes bad butter   1000

Scattering is easier than gathering   1001

The labour of the crow   1002

Put it on your shoulder and say it is not a burden   1003

It's no delay to stop to edge the tool   1004

The mason who strikes often is better than the
  one who strikes too hard   1005

It destroys the craft not to learn it   1006

The dog that's always on the go, is better than
  the one that's always curled up   1007

Handfulls make a load   1008

Don't go early or late to the well   1009

A good beginning is half the work   1010

Youth

TRIADS

Three as good as

Three things as good as the best; dirty water to quench a fire, a frieze coat on a frosty day and black bread in famine time.   1017

Three things that are as good as things better than them; a wooden sword in a coward's hand, an ugly wife married to a blind man and poor clothes on a drunken man.   1018

Three best

Three best friends and three worst enemies; fire, wind and rain.   1019

Three best to have in plenty; sunshine, wisdom and generosity.   1020

Three best things to have a surplus of; money after paying the rent, seed after spring and friends at home.   1021

Three best invitations; come to mass, come and make secure and come to the mill.   1022

Three with the best sight; the eye of a blacksmith on a nail, the eye of a young girl at a contest and the eye of a priest on his parish.   1023

Three best small; a beehive, a sheep and a woman   1024

The three best sounds; the sound of the flail, the sound of the quern, the sound of the churn.   1024a

Three fortunes

The three fortunes of the cat; the housewife's forgetfulness, walking without a sound, and keen sight in darkness.   1025

Three fortunes of the lucky man; fences,   1026
vigilance and early rising.

Three fortunes of the unlucky man; long visits   1027
to his neighbours, long morning sleep and
bad fences.

Three hardest

The three hardest to go through; a waterfall,   1028
a bog and a briary track.

The three hardest to select; a Sunday woman,   1029
an autumn sheep and an old mare's foal.

Three kinds

The three kinds of brain; brain as hard as stone,   1030
brain as receptive as wax and brain as
unstable as flowing water.

The three kinds of men; the worker, the pleasure-   1031
seeker and the boaster.

The three kinds of men who fail to understand   1032
women; young men, old men and middle-aged
men.

The three kinds of men who rise earliest; the   1033
husband of a talkative wife, the man with a
stolen white horse, and the man with a dirty
tattered shirt.

The three kinds of poor people; the man poor by   1034
the will of God, the man poor by his own will
and the man poor even if he owned the world.

The three kinds of women; the woman as   1035
shameless as a pig; the woman as unruly as a
hen and the woman as gentle as a lamb.

The three most

Three most bothersome things in the world;   1036
   a thorn in the foot, a woman and a goat going
   to the fair that will go anyway but the way you
   want it.

The three most delightful things to see; a garden   1037
   of white potatoes covered in blossom, a ship
   under sail and a woman after giving birth.

The three most difficult to select; a woman,   1038
   a scythe and a razor.

The three most difficult to teach; a mule, a pig   1039
   and a woman.

The three most difficult to understand; the   1040
   mind of a woman, the labour of the bees and
   the ebb and flow of the tide.

The three most fortunate things a man ever had;   1041
   a mare, a sow and a goose.

The three most nourishing foods; beef marrow,   1042
   the flesh of a chicken, Scandinavian beer.

The three most pleasant things; a cat's kitten,   1043
   a goat's kid and a young widow-woman.

The three most troubled eyes; the eye of a   1043a
   blacksmith after the nail; the eye of a
   chicken after the grain and the eye of a girl
   seeking her sweetheart.

Three traits

Three traits of a bull; a bold walk, a strong   1044
   neck and a hard forehead.

Three traits of a fox; a light step, a look to the   1045
   front and a glance to each side of the road.

Three traits of a hare; a lively ear, a bright eye
and a quick run against the hill.   1046

Three traits of a woman; a broad bosom, a
slender waist and a short back.   1047

Three ugliest

The three ugliest things that are; a hairless,
mangy dog, a woman without flesh or blood,
and a deceitful, shameless girl.   1048

The three ugliest things of their own kind; a thin
red-haired woman, a thin yellow horse and
a thin white cow.   1049

Three useless

The three things useless when old; an old
schoolmaster, an old horse and an old soldier.   1050

Three things that are of little use; a trumpet and
no tongue, a button and no buttonhole and a
wolf without teeth.   1051

Three worst

The three worst departures; leaving mass before
it ends, leaving table without grace and
leaving your wife to go to another woman.   1052

The three worst endings; the last days of a noble
old lady, the last days of an old white horse
and the last days of an old schoolmaster.   1053

The three worst endings; a house burning; a ship
sinking and an old white horse dying.   1053a

The three worst pets; a pet priest, a pet beggar
and a pet pig.   1054

The three worst things to have in a house;
a scolding wife, a smoky chimney and a leaky
roof.

1055

The three worse things of all; small, soft potatoes,
from that to an uncomfortable bed and to
sleep with a bad woman.

1056

Three things

Three things that cannot be acquired; voice,
generosity and poetry.

1057

Three things that arrive unnoticed; rent, age and
a beard.

1058

Three things to beware of; the hoof of the horse,
the horn of the bull and the smile of the Saxon.

1059

Three things a man should not boast of; the size
of his purse, the beauty of his wife and the
sweetness of his beer.

1060

Three things bright at first, then dull and finally
black; co-operation, a marriage alliance and
living in the one house.

1061

Three things Christ never intended; a woman
whistling, a hound howling and a hen crowing.

1062

Three things that relate to drink; to drink it,
to pay for it and to carry it.

1063

Three things that fill a haggard; ambition,
industry and constance vigilance.

1064

Three good things to have; a clean shirt, a clean
conscience and a guinea in the pocket.

1065

Three disagreeable things at home; a scolding
wife, a squalling child and a smoky chimney.

1066

Three things that don't bear nursing; an old
woman, a hen and a sheep.

1067

Three things that are purposeless; throwing a stone on a bend, giving advice to a wrathful woman, talking to a head without sense. 1068

Three things that remain longest in a family; fighting, red-hair and thieving. 1069

Three things that don't remain; a white cow, a handsome woman and a house on a height. 1070

Three things that can never return; a Sunday without mass, a day away from school and a day away from work. 1071

Three things that won't have rest; a steep waterfall, an otter, and a devil out of hell. 1072

Three things that never rust; a woman's tongue, the shoes of a butcher's horse and charitable peoples money. 1073

Three things that never rust; a sword, a spade and a thought. 1074

Three things never seen; a blade's edge, wind and love. 1075

Three sharpest things that are; a hound's tooth, a thorn in the mud and a fool's word. 1076

The three sharpest things; a fool's word, a thorn in the mud and a soft woollen thread that cuts to the bone. 1077

Three things that survive for the shortest time; a woman's association, the love of a mare for her foal and fresh oaten bread. 1078

Three things swiftest in the sea; the seal, the ray and the mackerel. 1079

Three things swiftest on land; the hound, the hare and the fox. 1080

Three things that leave the shortest traces; a bird on a branch, a ship on the sea and a man on a woman. 1081

Three things that leave the longest traces; charcoal on wood, a chisel on a block of stone and a ploughshare on a furrow. 1082

Three things not to be trusted; a fine day in winter, the life of an old person or the word of an important man unless it's in writing. 1083

Three things not be trusted; a cow's horn, a dog's tooth and a horse's hoof. 1084

Three things of least value in any house; too many geese in a house without a lake, too many women in a house without wool to be spun, too many horses in a house without ploughing to be done. 1085

Three things that have little value; the head of a woodcock, the head of a goat and the head of a gurnet. 1086

Three things a man should not be without; a cat, a chimney and a housewife. 1087

Miscellaneous

Three parts of the body most easily hurt; the knee, the elbow and the eye. — 1088

Three that do not clean their snouts; the farmer, the dog and the pig. — 1089

Three coldest things that are; a hound's snout, a man's knee and a woman's breast. — 1090

Three to whom it's little sense to pay a compliment; an old man, a bad man and a child. — 1091

Three deaths that ought not be bemoaned; the death of a fat hog, the death of a thief and the death of a proud prince. — 1092

Three the devil has without much trouble; the mason, the bailiff and the miller. — 1093

Three enemies of the body; wind, smoke and fleas. — 1094

Three errors relating to corn; to cut it green, to grind it damp and to eat it fresh. — 1095

Three great evils; smallness of house, closeness of heart and shortage of food. — 1096

Three with the sharpest eyes; a hawk on a tree, a fox in a glen, a young girl at a meeting. — 1097

Three wholesome foods for the driver; the back of a herring, the belly of a salmon and the head of a thrush (moorhen). — 1098

Three bad habits; drinking the glass, smoking the pipe and scattering the dew late at night. — 1099

Three happiest in the world; the tailor, the piper and the goat. — 1100

Three strokes that are keeping Ireland; the stroke of an axe on a block, of a hammer on an anvil and of a threshing flail in the center. — 1101

Three jobs that must be done with vigour; 1102
rowing, hammering and measuring the ground
with your fist (ie. using the sickle).

Three kind acts unrequited; that done for an old 1103
man, for a wicked person or for a little child.

Three sweetest melodies; the churning of butter, 1104
the plough ploughing and the mill grinding.

Three oaths that money swore; that it did not 1105
care who would possess it, that it would stay
but a while with any man and that it would
not stay with any man but the man who loved
it.

Three pair that never agree; two married women 1106
in the same house, two cats with one mouse
and two bachelors after the one young woman.

Three places that cannot be avoided; the place of 1107
birth, the place of death and the place of
burial.

Three times it is most likely to rain; early on 1108
Friday, late on Saturday and on Sunday
morning when it's time for first mass.

Three greatest rushes; the rush of water, the rush 1109
of fire and the rush of falsehood.

Three sauciest by nature; a ram, a bull and a 1110
tailor.

Three skills of the hare; sharp turning, high 1111
jumping, and strong running against the hill.

Three strongest forces; the force of fire, the 1112
force of water and the force of hatred.

Three truths; sunrise, sunset and death. 1113

Three unluckiest things to meet first thing in 1114
the morning; a mad dog, a man who lent you
money and a red-haired girl.

Three virtues of the drunkard; a miserable 1115
morning, a dirty coat and an empty pocket.

Three signs of an unfortunate man; going bail,   1115a
     intervening in disputes and giving evidence.

The three characteristics of the Fianna;   1115b
     purity of heart; strength of limb; and acting
     according to our word.

Four priests who are not greedy; four Frenchmen   1116
     who are not yellow (cowardly); four cobblers
     who don't tell lies; that's twelve not in this
     country.

Four things an Irishman should not trust;   1117
     a cow's horn, a horse's hoof, a dog's snarl
     and an Englishman's laugh. (Compare 1059)

The four fortunes of the cat; the housewife's   1118
     error; walking without care; no water in milk,
     and sight at night as well as by day.
     (Compare 1025)

Four hateful things: a worthless hound,   1119
     a slow horse, a chief without wisdom
     and a wife without children.

NOTES

Proverbs 50 & 707

The buailtin is the part of the flail that strikes the corn.

Proverb 51

Ciotog is the Irish word for a left-handed person; it often implies awkwardness. In this instance, however, the implication is one of cuteness or guile. Various superstitions have been associated with the ciotog—including suspicion of evil or treachery (Note the English word 'sinister', from the latin).

Proverb 55

The Irish word 'meitheal' means a team of workers (neighbours) assisting one another at turf-cutting or hay-making. The blacksmith usually had the largest meitheal in the parish since his work at the forge was of such importance to the community.

Proverb 60

'The Old Woman of Beare'—a legendary figure in Irish folklore and poetry. (See Padraic Pearse's poem, *Mise Eire*, and Austin Clarke's, *The Young Woman of Beare*).

Proverb 71

About 300 a.d. when Corman MacArt was High King of Ireland, ruling from Tara, a warrior army called the Fianna was formed under the leadership of Fionn MacCumhaill. Around the Fianna and its leader grew a great body of legend still popular today. Fionn himself was noted for his bravery and wisdom (he tasted the salmon of knowledge). The Fianna eventually became too powerful for the High King but were defeated at the battle of Gabhra and disbanded.

Proverb 203a

The word 'cess', according to P. W. Joyce, may mean a contraction of success, or a 'contribution'. He refers to its use in County Louth as meaning a quantity of corn in for threshing.

Proverb 271
Lough Sheelin is a large lake in County Cavan

Proverb 441
Used as a reply when you are reminded by someone of a favour he has granted you.

Proverb 595 & 598
'Speckled' refers to the 'heat-spots' got on the shins from sitting too long and too close by the fire.

Proverb 716
This proverb is King Diarmuid's famous judgement, given about 560 a.d., on the ownership of a manuscript copy made by St Colmcille of a manuscript belonging to St Finnian. It must be one of our first copyright laws.

INDEX

INDEX

116

INDEX

118

119

121

INDEX

122

Books from Wolfhound Press

for YOUNG READERS: two titles by Liam O'Flaherty:

ALL THINGS COME OF AGE:

a rabbit story

ISBN 0 905473 08 6. Boards 22x15 illustrations by
Terence O'Connell; £1.50.

A sensitive, gently told story about nature and survival its cha-
acters are a baby rabbit. its mother a wicked-eyed weasel. A
beautiful and classic tale. full of the emotions. mystery. magic
and reality of nature.

THE TEST OF COURAGE

ISBN 0 905473 06 X. Boards 22x15 illustrations by
Terence O'Connell; £1.50.

This is one of Liam O'Flaherty's finest stories about children, and
is ideal reading for young people aged 8+. Michael O'Hara and
Peter Cooke, two young island boys set out for night's bream fish-
ing in a stolen curragh. In the darkness they drift, unawares, out
to sea . . .

The Wolfhound Book of Irish Poems for Young People

Selected by Bridie Quinn
& Seamus Cashman

A wide-ranging collection of
poems by Irish poets, selected for the young. A dual-
purpose book, for education
and for pleasure; for the
young person and for the ad-
ult poetry reader too.

'This book cannot be too
highly recommended . . . a
treasure and a treasury.
Irish Press

'Admirable in concept, selec-
tion and presentation . . . it
is also admirable value for in
addition to the 139 works it
embraces, it has explanatory
notes, brief biographies of the
poets, photographs and a number of excellent drawings . . .'
Irish Independent

192 pages; 35 drawings and
photos.

Liam O'Flaherty

SKERRETT

Skerrett is a powerful and vigorous novel. Set in the western island of 'Nara' (the Aran Islands), it has been acclaimed as Liam O'Flaherty's best-written book.

It is the story of David Skerrett — a man stripped of everything he possesses until he stands alone in a tiny cabin by the edge of the sea. Skerrett is a solitary, alienated hero seeking his identity; in turn, village schoolmaster and village idiot; now tender, now violent, now frenzied: 'I defy them all. They can't make me bend the knee.'

Nara, the island to which Skerrett and his pregnant wife, Kate, are driven by an ill-fate, is a place where a whole village can erupt in a frenzy of excitement at a good catch of fish; where instability turns friend into foe, foe into friend with startling suddeness. Its people are a peasant people, dominated by Moclair, the 'subtle priest' whose challenge turns Skerrett, from being a reformer, into a revolutionary...

Case bound; 210 x 140
288 pages; £4.50 net.

SKERRETT

THE
PEDLAR'S
REVENGE
and other stories

LIAM O'FLAHERTY

The Pedlar's Revenge bears the hall mark of one of this century's great short story writers. O'Flaherty ranges effortlessly from earthy to lyrical. from the creatures of field and shore to gaunt studies of the meaning of courage and caustic treatment of embottled brawlers. Like Synge he can ring carillons from everyday peasant speech, but he is above all a marvellously visual writer who prints his descriptions on the retina ; a field of wheat rippling like a pegged-down carpet, a miser forcibly purged after swallowing his last coin to spite his

Guardian

All in all, then, a thoroughly fascinating and thought-provoking collection of stories. Mr. O'Flaherty's latest story, 'Wild Stallions' is as strongly structured and faultless as the tales of his youth, giving proof, if proof were needed, that the old artificer has lost none of his skill in the intervening years. I salute him.

Independent

IT IS timely that yet another generation should discover Liam O'Flaherty. Since his first collection " Spring Sowing " came out in 1924 he has been accounted as one of the masters of the short story.

Survival and courage are his themes—both in nature and in man. Whether he is writing of donkeys or drakes. crows or rabbits, Aran fishermen, floods, hatred, love, revenge, peasants, drunks or children. he is capable of the most searchingly accurate observation, tender but never sentimental.

An old woman is speaking to an old man, once her lover; " Every bit of it is plain to me." she says, " alive as a blister." Or, when he is describing an animal pound, " the ground within this circular enclosure was as naked as a monk's skull."

"The Pedlar's Revenge" contains 21 stories, all except two published in magazines over the last 40 years, but hitherto uncollected. What a refreshment they are. A. A. Kelly has chosen them and contributed an evocative and valuable introduction

Daily Telegraph

Dunsany
957 Slane
s Ledwidge
917 Slane

ctive

MEATH

Higgins
Celbridge

E   R

chard Power
28-1970 Naas

RE

Dublin City

DUBLIN

John Millington Synge
1871-1909 (b. Dublin)

WI   LOW

Francis Stuart
1902 —— Laragh
(b.Australia)

DUBLIN CITY

Samuel Beckett
1906 ——
Brendan Behan
1923-1964
Dion Boucicault
1822-1890
Austin Clarke
1896-1974
Brian Coffey
1905 ——
Denis Devlin
1908-1959 (b. Scotland)
Monk Gibbon
1896 ——
Oliver St. John Gogarty
1878-1957
Valentin Iremonger
1918 ——
Denis Johnston
1901 ——
James Joyce
1882-1941
Thomas Kinsella
1928 ——
Joseph Sheridan Le Fanu
1814-1873
Charles Lever
1806-1872
Samuel Lover
1797-1868
amah Mac Donagh

A LITERARY MAP OF IRELAND
Coloured Poster   Size: c. 830 x 450
Containing the names, dates and place of birth
or association, of c. 150 of the principle Irish writers,   ngan
with decorations relating to the literature, and por-
traits. Compiled by Maurice Harmon, MRIA, and
designed by Jarlath and Susan Hayes.

—1964
Eimar O'Duffy
1893-1935
Seamus O'Sullivan
1879-1958
Padraic Pearse
1879-1916
James Plunkett